Big Teddy has lived in the toyshop for a long time and there is nothing he wants more than to find a new home...

Big Teddy

A Bedtime Story

by Lilian Murray
illustrated by Gill Guile

Copyright © 1991 by World International Publishing Limited.
All rights reserved.
Published in Great Britain by World International Publishing Limited,
An Egmont Company, Egmont House, P.O.Box 111,
Great Ducie Street, Manchester M60 3BL.
Printed in DDR. ISBN 0 7498 0066 6

A CIP catalogue record for this book is available from the British Library

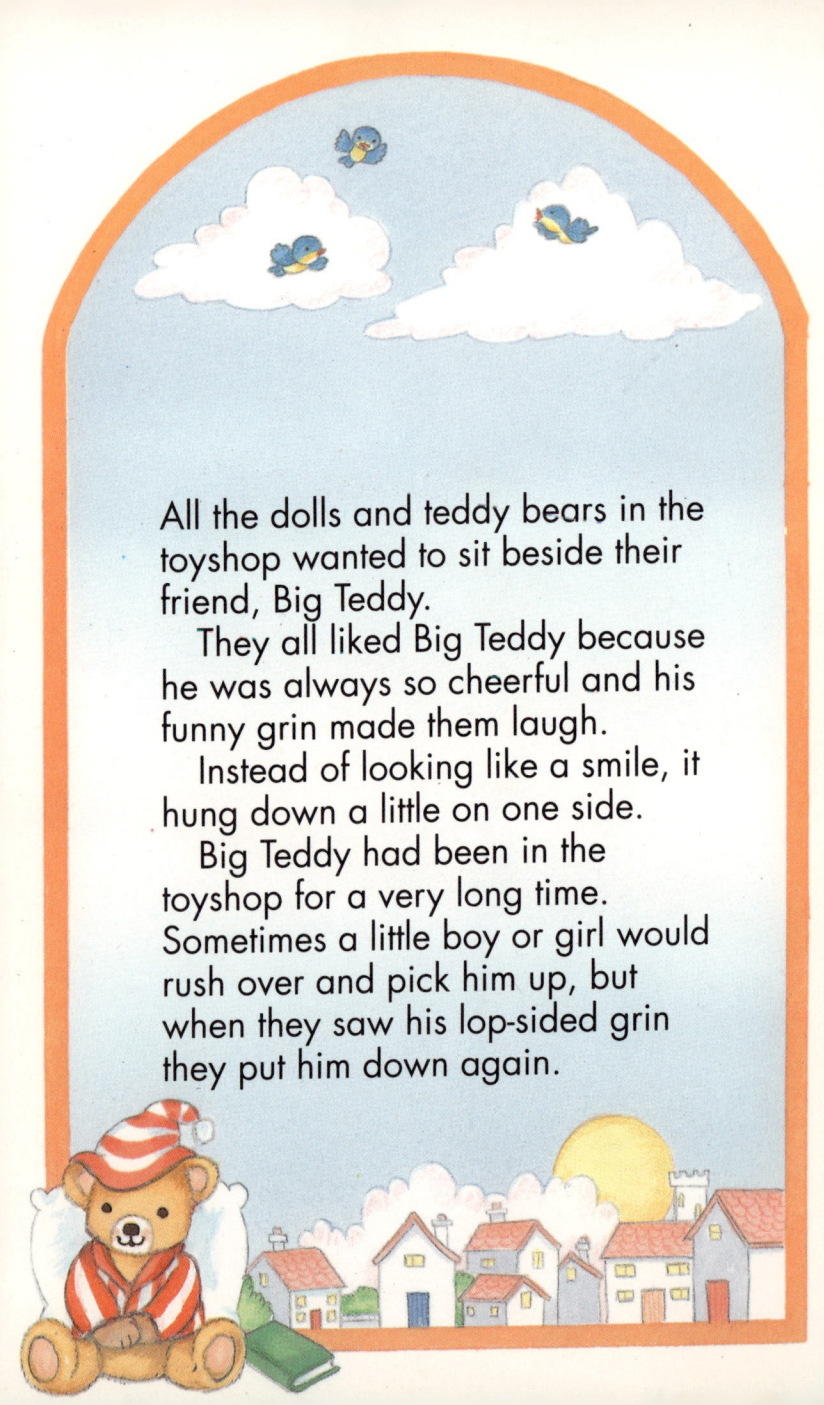

All the dolls and teddy bears in the toyshop wanted to sit beside their friend, Big Teddy.

They all liked Big Teddy because he was always so cheerful and his funny grin made them laugh.

Instead of looking like a smile, it hung down a little on one side.

Big Teddy had been in the toyshop for a very long time. Sometimes a little boy or girl would rush over and pick him up, but when they saw his lop-sided grin they put him down again.

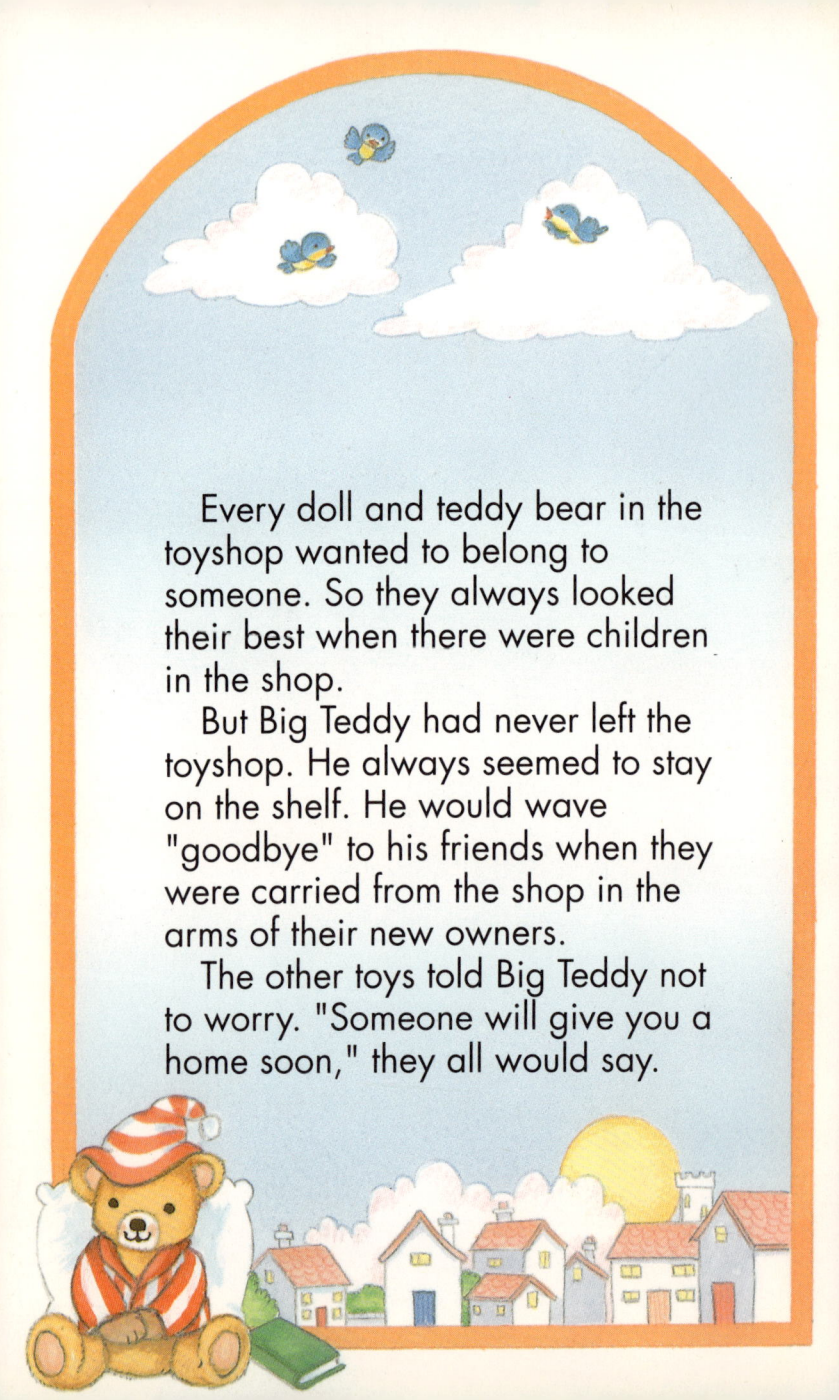

Every doll and teddy bear in the toyshop wanted to belong to someone. So they always looked their best when there were children in the shop.

But Big Teddy had never left the toyshop. He always seemed to stay on the shelf. He would wave "goodbye" to his friends when they were carried from the shop in the arms of their new owners.

The other toys told Big Teddy not to worry. "Someone will give you a home soon," they all would say.

Big Teddy began to look quite untidy after a long time in the toyshop.

A small hole had appeared in his right leg and his sawdust stuffing had started to fall out.

When the children saw this, they stopped picking Big Teddy up.

To keep cheerful, Big Teddy sang this little song:

"Mustn't grumble,
Can't complain.
Soon I'll have a new home,
Then I'll smile again."

Then one day the shopkeeper saw some of Big Teddy's sawdust stuffing on the floor.

"What a mess!" she cried. "Where is it coming from?"

She walked around the toyshop and shook each teddy bear. None of them lost any sawdust.

Then she picked up Big Teddy. Out fell some sawdust.

"It's *you*, Big Teddy! How can I sell you with a hole in your leg?" asked the shopkeeper. "You'll have to go!"

All the other toys watched as their friend was taken outside.

"It's no good, Big Teddy," said the shopkeeper, gently. "You've been in the toyshop long enough. With a hole in your leg, who will want you?"

The shopkeeper took the lid off a dustbin and dropped Big Teddy head first inside.

A trail of sawdust led all the way from the shop to the dustbin.

"What a mess!" the shopkeeper said. "What a messy mess!"

"Golleee!" sighed Big Teddy. "It's very dark in here...but I really mustn't grumble."

Through a hole in the side of the dustbin, Big Teddy watched as the shopkeeper swept all his sawdust stuffing off the garden path.

Then Big Teddy heard the sound of the toys in the toyshop crying. So he sang them another little song:

"Who fell in
The old dustbin?
It's only Big Teddy
Standing on his heady!"

All that day Big Teddy stood on his head inside the dark dustbin.

Through the hole in the side of the dustbin he could see children leaving the toyshop carrying their new toys.

"Oh, who will ever want me now?" cried Big Teddy to himself. "My stuffing is falling out and I don't look as good as I used to."

Then Big Teddy heard the sound of a lorry. It stopped nearby and through his spy-hole Big Teddy could see someone approaching.

Suddenly the dustbin lid was lifted off and a voice shouted, "Hey, look what I've found!"

A hand reached inside and pulled Big Teddy out by his feet.

Big Teddy had been found by the dustbinmen!

"I like his lop-sided grin," said one of the dustbinmen.

"Makes me feel cheerful," said another. "He doesn't belong in a dustbin, does he? He could be our lucky mascot! Let's keep him!"

Big Teddy smiled his funny smile.

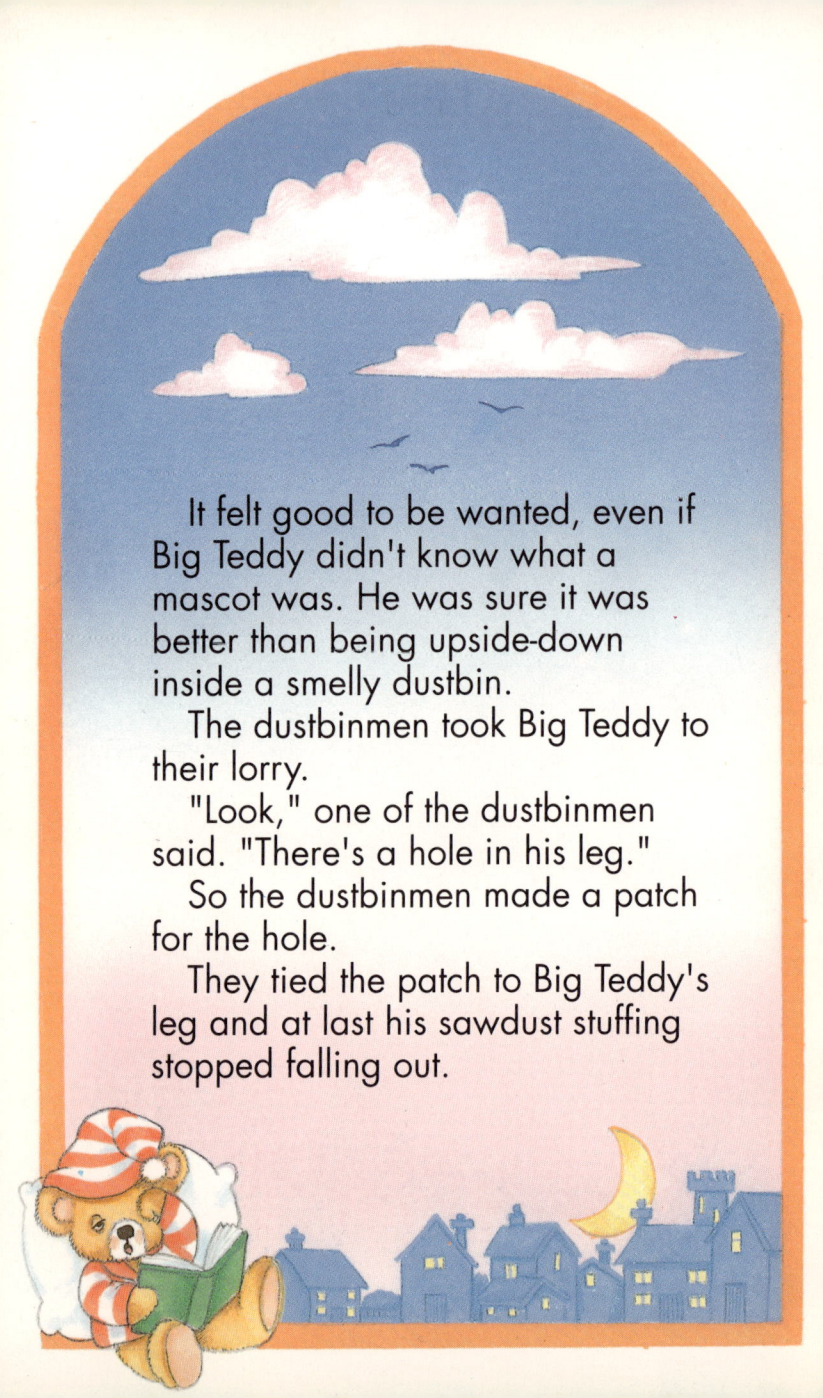

It felt good to be wanted, even if Big Teddy didn't know what a mascot was. He was sure it was better than being upside-down inside a smelly dustbin.

The dustbinmen took Big Teddy to their lorry.

"Look," one of the dustbinmen said. "There's a hole in his leg."

So the dustbinmen made a patch for the hole.

They tied the patch to Big Teddy's leg and at last his sawdust stuffing stopped falling out.

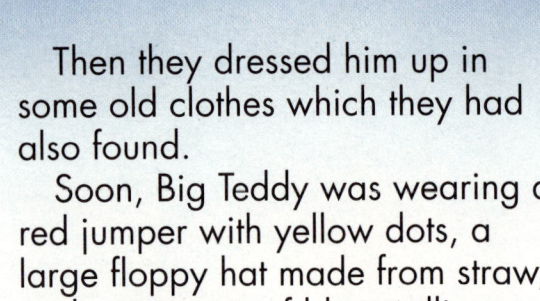

Then they dressed him up in some old clothes which they had also found.

Soon, Big Teddy was wearing a red jumper with yellow dots, a large floppy hat made from straw, and a tiny pair of blue wellington boots.

The dustbinmen held a mirror in front of Big Teddy. He looked so different!

"Oh! Ha! Ha!" he chuckled. "How funny I look! I'll make everyone laugh!"

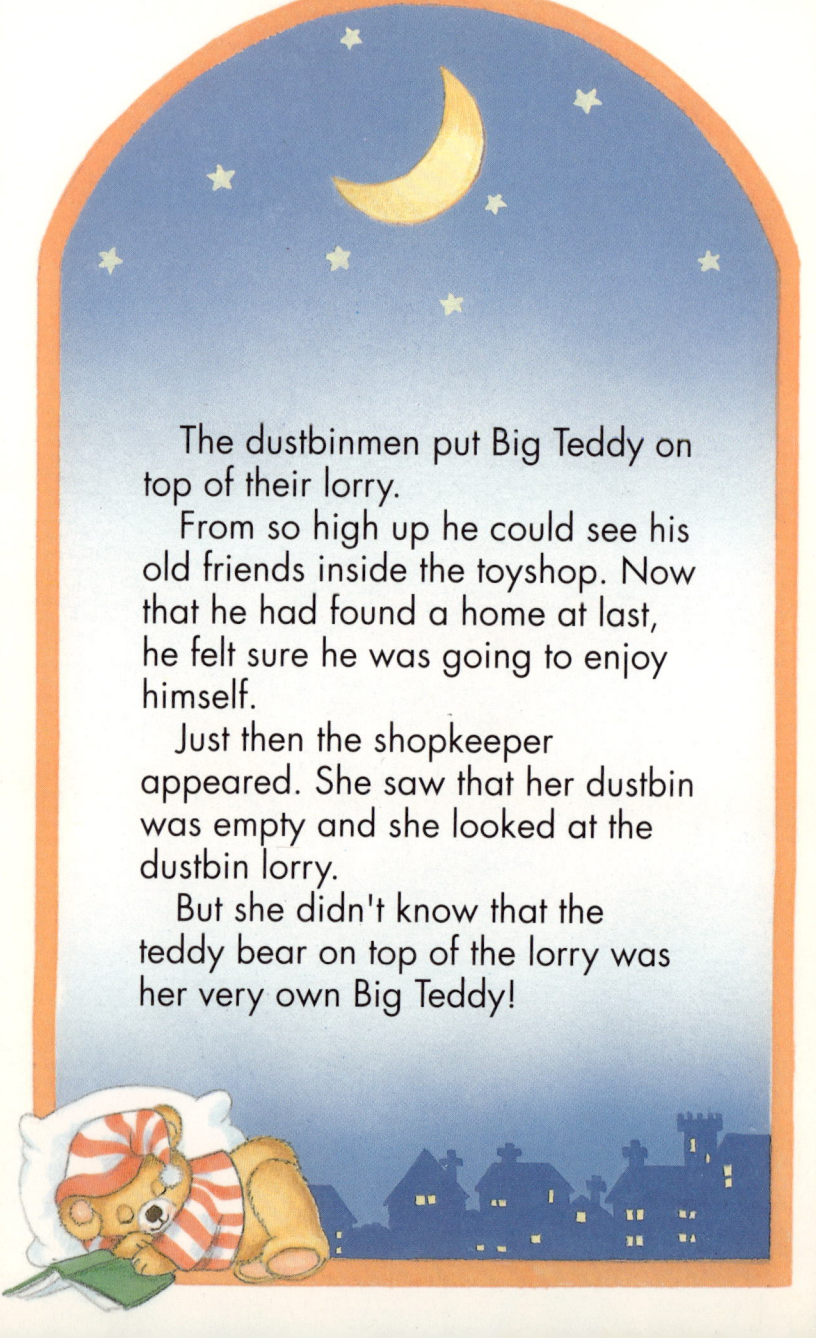

The dustbinmen put Big Teddy on top of their lorry.

From so high up he could see his old friends inside the toyshop. Now that he had found a home at last, he felt sure he was going to enjoy himself.

Just then the shopkeeper appeared. She saw that her dustbin was empty and she looked at the dustbin lorry.

But she didn't know that the teddy bear on top of the lorry was her very own Big Teddy!

Off went the lorry and Big Teddy waved "goodbye" to his friends.

They were so pleased he had found a new home at last.

Big Teddy could see lots of children in the streets.

They laughed when they saw him, and they must have liked his lop-sided grin because they joined in with his happy little song:

"Mustn't grumble,
Can't complain.
If you look on the bright side,
The sun will shine again!"